Some Kind of Miracle

Poems by Paul Stokstad

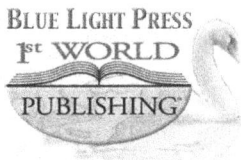

BLUE LIGHT PRESS
1st WORLD
PUBLISHING

San Francisco | Fairfield | Delhi

Some Kind of Miracle

Paul Stokstad

Copyright ©2020 by Paul Stokstad

First Edition.

ISBN: 978-1-4218-3658-4

Library of Congress Control Number: 2020937606

1ST WORLD LIBRARY
PO Box 2211
Fairfield, Iowa 52556
www.1stworldpublishing.com

BLUE LIGHT PRESS
www.bluelightpress.com
Email: bluelightpress@aol.com

Contents

THE HOUSE

THE US

THE KEY

THE LOVE

THE END

LAGNIAPPPE

THE HOUSE

It's 5 a.m.

And out on the lawn
in the gathering cold,
one of the fallen leaves
dark, against the
sodden grass,
lies silent, in decay
and yet, on this
December morning,
still sparkles
with frost.

The Tree Out Back

Not sure why
the tree out back
after holding tightly on
to its leafy clothes
through hot calm
and blowing wet,

With the advent of
frozen white
lightly strips off
in a slow-motion fall
her tiny veils
and stands,
black, naked
against the winter.

And then you see
all the hands
all the fingers
that it takes
to make her
so big, so beautiful

The Morning Fog

The morning fog
like a grey fur
lays over
and erases
the fields
around our home,
the corn disappearing
in a soft exchange of
green for grey.

But that's not the thing today,
it's the fact of looking,
of seeing,
of having eyes,
this way of knowing
that there are objects
near and far.

On most days
the buildings and trees
off to the west,
and today
the blueberry powder
in the cupboard,
the oatmeal steaming.

Pause

The sun reaches
across the floor.

Upstairs the washer
is working hard.

It's Wednesday, the 8th day
of November.

There's a little pause
right now,

before everything.

Earlier today

Earlier today
our backyard tree
stood, naked of leaves,
against a cold, grey sky
but just now,
it was quickly
and briefly dressed,
by a polka dot collection
of singing birds.

If you put a seed

If you put a seed
in the ground,
dark forces gather,
dusky minerals flow,
water comes.

The deep dark
holds that seed,
feeds it, brings what it needs
to swell a bit
to take those elements,
those aspects
of what we call dirt
and convert them into cell and sprout,
reach up to the light
and then, breaking out,
but still holding firm
and rooting deeper,
into a firmer, finer relationship,
into the dark source,
to then stretch
flowering to the light.

The front lawn,
these trees,
the last flowers of the season
here like clothing
for a deep, dark nourishing earth.

The Day after Christmas

Today the cats
wander the house
wishing for different weather

they ask us to
open the door
now and then
maybe thinking that

one more time
when we do
somehow it will be better

little do they know
that it is the day
after Christmas

and it is the law
that little or nothing
can happen today

THE US

Tuesday Night

tuesday night
all my dear ones
fast asleep

a cold night before
a cold winter

one thing I'd like
to mention is

that if we ever met
or even if
we haven't

thanks for sharing
this planet,
this time,
this air

It's 5:19 am

So many of you are still asleep
some in dreams,
some in silence
and some awake inside,
in an enlightened quiet.

Here and there,
on this continent
people that I loved,
and still love,
now sleeping with new loves,
new lives
not yet in daylight,
but still in grateful memory.

And some others,
asleep to this world
yet awake in another
mystic place, sort through
day by day, love by love
what they gave or gained
and plan their next earthly move.

This or that planet
this or that star
awake or not
with living beings.

Somewhere another soul
up early in an alien morning,
wondering who else is up and awake
in the interstellar night.

Tending the Fire

Even though I sit alone
in this room, in the early morning
I can feel that you are with me.

Sitting up or standing, walking,
sleeping or meditating, right now

That I am not the only one
carefully tending this delicate flame
of consciousness, every day,
feeding it the best fuel
in terms of pure intention
foods that support more mental clarity
exercise, maybe even asanas,
pranayama, abhyanga, panchakarma,
or any other Sanskrit words
that we can find, to light the fire
with tinder, a delicate breath,

Encouraging a spark of awareness to light,
building up a full bonfire, until such a time when
an inner light is on every day, every minute,
every second, and even in the deep night
you and I, together, illuminated within
enlighten even a sleeping body
a slumbering town, a world that is still
just now waking.

You might not know

You might not know
when you think of me
that, sorting laundry,
I make two piles,
one for the dresser,
and one for the closet.

That I'm not much of a cook
but do scrub pots and tools,
fill and empty the dishwasher.

You may not know
that I take out the trash,
make our bed,
feed the finicky cats,
and add gas to the car

There may seem to be
nothing special in these acts,

But I am grateful to be
with all of you
as we do them.

Message to Poets

–For Bill Graeser

I have nothing to say to you,
but know that
I don't have to say it,
because you are
already in touch
with nothing.

Since it seems that
nothing is the message
in almost every poem
no, not that nothing:

the deep, silent, full nothing
that is at the basis of everything.

You are not my audience
(what can I tell you?)

It's for others who think
they can't write a poem,
but can read and be reminded
of nothing,
in the middle of a busy day,
and in that silence,
smile.

Miracle

Everywhere that you went today
there was a sort of miracle.

I suppose you missed it
(most people do).

It had trillions of cells,
seventy-eight organs
and forty-six miles of nerves,
carrying messages at 170 mph.

Without thinking about it,
it could breathe, pump
blood, process lunch
and make cells
while the sun shone.

It could feel, think, remember,
speak, read, write, and respond.

It could probably reach out
and touch, feel the heat,
It possibly walked, leaned,

crawled out or into bed.
It learned, watched, thought,
smelled or tasted.

and maybe, hopefully
loved.

Really, there was
some kind of miracle
all day, wherever
you were

No More

no more men
or women
just people

no more french toast
just toast
fried with egg

no german
chocolate cake
it's now chocolate
cake with coconut

no more definitives
just infinitives

nothing decisive
only insightful

no labels to define
just things to
refine

If I'm in love with you
it's you, me
and the love

that's it.

In My Next War

In my next war
it will be dish against dish
falafel and tahini
against kreplach soup.

If you want to have a war
you have to show up at the border
with your best dishes,
and those other people come
with their pans and sauces,
you sample and sniff, back and forth,

and then agree, yes, you really have a point
with that baklava, and yes,
that curry with peas and panir
offers a fresh perspective
(I hadn't thought of that).

Then, if you want to be a terrorist
you have to set up a table, in a crowd
and then surprise everyone
with a burst of flavors, from the old country
suhur, and later, das bil hamof.

That's my kind of war.

Cat Love

You just can't feel
someone else's love

It can't be slathered
on and around you, like butter,
so you are encased in it.

But you can love and feel love
for another, and they can feel
the same for you.

So, when I say
I love you
It's that I feel love
around you,
I am filled with love
because of you
and I am in love,
my own love,
due to you.

So, the next time
you think nobody loves me
you might start by
feeling love for yourself,
because what's nice about a cat
is not so much the cat licking
but the cat purring.

In this love

Imagine with me,
that as you move
within the room or space
that you are in
right now, look to the left,
pick something up, and stop,

That you move through love,
walk through love, and that every move,
turn, thought, and action
is admired, lovingly filmed,

That an eternal record
follows each of your moments,
that someone, you, me,
your mother, somebody,
is watching, and adores
everything that you do, and are.

And then, holding that as real,
you now enter into the ceremony,
the beauty, the miracle
that you were, are, and always will be,
here on this earth, in this time,
in this love.

No Rush

don't be
in a hurry

because you
can't be
in a hurry

since when
you are
in a hurry

there's no you
and no being

just hurry

WHITE SUPREMACY

I don't know where they got that idea.

It's not in the rainbow.
It's the color of bones.

If it's paper, it means you can't think
of anything to write.

It's the kind of scratchy shirt you wear
to Sunday school.

If it's a pill it means, at least
you have a headache.

As crackers go, it's dry and tasteless.

It can't even jump off the page.

It's the only shade of ghosts.
It's crack, meth, or coke.
It's the kind of sheet that fear is as.

It's worse than burnt sienna,
madder lake, and raw umber, since
there's no crayon for people of no color.

Oh yes white has its problems.
it makes supreme a sea of hate

And, did I mention that
its not even in the rainbow?

If I haven't thanked you yet

If I haven't thanked you yet
for sharing this language
let me thank you now.

With you I can easily say
and have you hear
that I am grateful for you
for all you do
to exist on this planet,
in your body:
the feeding, the cleaning,
the dressing, exercising,
study, work, talk, love and dance,

Such that when I say thank you
not just for reading, but for being
in this world with me
and roll a sort of golden marble
of feeling your way
in the form of this poem
you are there to pick it up,
see and feel.

THE KEY

The Key

Despite all the clues
Very few will ever find this page, this space.

Thanks be given, you made it thus far.

If you take anything from this dream
remember, when you leave, to take

this key.

These are the instructions:

Now that you have the key
You may travel deep inside

On the way in, you may pass
place names in stone,
directional signs,
maps from previous explorers.
Never mind these, keep going.

You will know the way by the light
of love, glowing within.

Beyond all, there is
what we could call a lake
both valuable and shining
though no word is light enough
to guide you there
or big enough to hold it
on the way back out.

You can drop this key
as you enter the bright water.

What you'll find is
only what you really are
and will be,
from this day onward.

THE LOVE

Barely day

I open one eye,
and see her in the dark,
gliding over
to the dresser, the closet.
one last time,
and then out the door,
off to work.

Small, slender,
she moves through the room
and my grateful heart.

The Pie

It may not be
believable to some,
but I really did debate
whether to eat
the last bite of the pie
you sent with me today,
or to leave it be
and at least
for some time
treasure the curve
of the crust that, after all
your tiny hands had pressed
deep into the corners
of our glass baking dish.

You can do no wrong

Whatever you do
is purified by your presence.

Whatever you see
is enlightened by your vision.

Whatever you love
is exalted by your heart.

Whatever you touch
is sanctified by your skin.

Whatever you decide
where you go, who you see
help, uplift, and hold,

This love follows, fills and adores
your every thought and action.

You can do no wrong.

A thousand tears

I would drop a thousand
tears

Rather than see your face with
one

I only ever wanted to bring you
smiles

little candies outside your
door

and dance songs to
try

Please let me cry all the
tears

and save all the smiles, just in
case

you need chase a tear
away

I'm grateful

I'm grateful for
another day,
your voice on the phone,
ninety miles away.

I'm grateful for
your call, checking in,
reporting on your day.

I'm grateful for
your bedroom, decorated with
reminders of the divine.

I'm grateful standing here
In your closet,
your clothing, folded, stored,
though somedays lucky
worn next to your museum quality,
live and breathing body, filled with light.

I'm grateful for
your patience, when I get lost
in maybes, to bring me back
to now.

I'm grateful for you, still
here in the high waves,
and how you say
see me, feel my hand
in yours, and my heart with you,
from any time and distance, forever.

Every day

Every day with you
is a precious gift,

An exquisite, gilded
ancient, Fabergé egg,
priceless within a glass case.

Every day a precious gift,

An exotic, unnamed flower
opening once, alone,
revealing an unearthly beauty,
while releasing a divine scent
into the jungle.

Every day with you a gift,

Like waking up in a monastery
to the sound of a single bell
and for a long moment
there is no thought
of where and when
just being.

Every day precious,
knowing that
I'm either going
to die soon,
you will be leaving,
or each moment
is the only place
where we ever really meet.

THE END

When People Die

When people die, we gather,
we think of them, of what they did for us
and others, of how they talked,
their knowing look, as they left the room,
or told a joke, the selfless giving,
the unaccountably kind gesture.

And it's not really clear
how the living room will even work
without that familiar piece of furniture.

We want to say stop, it doesn't make sense
to go on, but we do, and after a few days
the roll of lunches, bills, and cleaning up continues.

Still, let me tell you now that I appreciate you,
You who are reading this

All you do to give; all you mean to me or others

Let us all remember and recognize you now
while you are in the body, can read this and know

You are loved, admired, treasured, and deeply valued.
Even if our parting this time is not a death
but just the fact that you have left the room
for a moment.

Last Day

In the evening of Dad's last day
I fed him peas and carrots.

He didn't like the chocolate Ensure.

I sang "Just a closer walk with thee"
and Mary hugged him.

Then some people we didn't know showed up,
And he led an animated talk
about their athletic daughter,
after which he tired
and we left him to sleep.

Then at 2 am we got the call, and
we took that first time ever last drive,
for which there is no training
to see what was left of him.

and sister Mary took a few snips
of dear grey hair
for each of us to keep.

For Finn

When you walk off the dock
and die,
you sink beneath the water
and the part of the dock
closest to land
separates from the end
and floats away
and then there is a gap between the shore
and the remaining dock, out there
and we cannot follow you

When you walk off the dock,
because that is your purpose
and die,
we stand by the shore
in wonder that
you have sunk out of sight

It's not that we can rescue you.
Rescue efforts were made, long ago,
but we can wonder about the fact
that there is water, dock, but no you

When you die, you are as if gone,
Underwater,
and when we walk by the lake, later,
we see the broken dock
but not you

Still, one thing you may not
have known
when you walked off
is that we own this water
we know this water.
Even here on shore
we are deeply connected
to all water

And not only that,
we are part of all the earth
that holds all water
in its palm

So, when you seem to disappear
from view,
you are not lost to us
except for in the dry air
of daily living

Wherever you are floating
underwater
in the deep,
we are that deep.
We are with you in that
wet and full level
of coexistence

We hold you in our deep
dark, divine palm of love
and we never let go.
We never agree that you are gone,
just changed from living
in our visible love
to our invisible love
forever.

When the Walls of the Museum Fall

–For Fred Rosenberg

When the walls of the museum fall,
like the one with the intelligent face
and amused smile of this, our Frederick,
(whose name after all means king of peace)
then we look to the space left behind.

When the walls of the museum fall
and we, still in the building
have a faraway look,

It's just that when something
as great and so much a part of us
as this has fallen,

That now it seems
it's all space,
we are all space
there are no walls
and nothing has fallen
but opened.

Sometimes I wonder

Sometimes I wonder
If there may be
A last flower seen up close
A last time hearing something by Leonard Cohen
A last laugh due to Bertie and Jeeves
A last tennis ball hit just out of reach,

Or a last day, like this day,

The last day, when, after the fire drill
At the nursing home, my sister Jan
Went into her room and lay down, to a final breath,

And then became blue flows of water,
red, purifying flame, and a sort of free
unearthly laughter,

Conveying thanks to those that loved her,
comfort for those in loss, concern for things
she missed doing,

But mostly freedom,
pure freedom

Mourning after

When the ceremonies
are over,
When the photos have been
gathered up
off the reception table
and the leftover cookies
taken home
by the last person,
and long after
the janitor comes
through the room, sweeping,

Yes, maybe months later,
while cleaning my room
I pick up something
with your name on it, then
even though I was calm
through all the memorials,
and following weeks,
then, it will be a sort of
simple thing, me right here,
and you out there, somewhere,
and when no one knows,

and all have moved on,
then is when my
lonesome tear may fall.

LAGNIAPPE

Reputation

I have to apologize
if I ever thought of a phrase
that would make a punchline
of your straight line.

Yes, there may be people
who think of me as funny
or witty, and even though
at one time I may have liked that
to them I apologize.

That was not what my mother hoped for me.

I have to apologize
if ever I shared
some idea or plan
that appeared to be superior,
for some marketing
or work situation.

And yes, there may be
some people who
think of me as insightful,

and even though
I may have wished
for such a reputation,

That is not what I learned from my mother.

There may be some at work
who nodded their heads
when I noted some apparently
stupid corporate decision.

And even though some
may have seen me as their friend
and not the boss'.

That was not her wish for me.

For sometimes a joke
may have hurt someone,
or made light of something
that needed attention,

And sometimes my idea
may have eclipsed
a better one
from a less noisy person,

And sometimes a leader
had more people
and things to balance t
han I could know.

If ever you knew me
for anything else, I apologize,
for the only thing
that I know my mother wished for me
was that I bring love
into the world
and that I would somehow
be a force for good.

So, at this late date
let me mention
the love
that all this time
I meant to bring you,
the love
I was supposed to offer you,
And the love
that is all I hope to leave.

The situation

Looking at the situation
right now
there are a few concerns:

Possible death,
a pandemic or two,
destruction of health,
loss of home,
our future together,
friends and neighbors dying,
civil war,
the ongoing inanity
of a chief executive,
and a tv-only football season.

So, let me note
that just now
every good day with you
is a golden jewel
laid on the table
in morning light.

And every
heart-filled moment
my version of
heaven on earth.

We don't know
the future,
but we do know
this love, this day.

About the Author

Paul Stokstad is a work in progress, which has included, and still includes, at various stages of construction, improv theatre, tennis, college teaching, linguistics, musical theatre, disco, stand up comedy, the TM Program, and time spent in the love lost and found. He inherited poetry from his mother and crowd control from his father. Everything else came due to the kindness of former strangers, or he simply made it up. He does put a lot of attention on words, but he is even more fond of silence, and its home in the space that holds all creativity, love and possibility: the now.

Books by Paul Stokstad

Some Kind of Miracle
Butterfly Tattoo
How to Start Your Own Improv Comedy Group
How to Be your Own Best Tennis Pro

Ebooks:
The Map of Iowa
Voice of Reason, Election 2016

www.ingramcontent.com/pod-product-compliance
Lightning Source LLC
Chambersburg PA
CBHW032029090426
42741CB00006B/793